Austra
Travel Guide

BRISBANE

Exploring Brisbane City
(Australia's Vibrant Gem)

Chase Faxon

Copyright © 2023 by Chase Faxon

This book is a work of nonfiction. The information and opinions expressed in this book are solely those of the author and do not necessarily represent the views or opinions of any individuals or organizations mentioned within.

Table of Contents:

Introduction

Chapter One: Getting to Know Brisbane
- Overview of Brisbane
- History and Culture
- Climate and Best Time to Visit
- Getting Around Brisbane

Chapter Two: Exploring Brisbane
- 1. City Center and Central Business District (CBD)
- 2. Queen Street Mall
- 3. South Bank Parklands
- 4. Kangaroo Point
- 5. Cultural and Historical Sites
- 6. Brisbane City Hall
- 7. Queensland Museum and Sciencentre
- 8. The Story Bridge
- 9. Nature and Outdoor Activities
- 10. Lone Pine Koala Sanctuary
- 11. Mount Coot-tha
- 12. Moreton Island
- 13. Dining and Nightlife
- 14. Fortitude Valley
- 15. Eagle Street Pier
- 16. Eat Street Northshore
- 17. Shopping and Markets
- 18. Queen Street Mall

- 19. James Street
- 20. South Bank Lifestyle Markets

Chapter Three: Day Trips from Brisbane
- 1. Gold Coast
- 2. Sunshine Coast
- 3. Byron Bay
- 4. Lamington National Park
- 5. Noosa Heads

Chapter Four: Accommodation Options
- Hotels and Resorts
- Hostels and Budget Accommodation
- Apartment Rentals

Chapter Five: Practical Information
- Local Cuisine and Restaurants
- Shopping Tips
- Language and Communication
- Health and Safety

Conclusion
- Final Thoughts

Travel Tracker Notebook Journal

Introduction

Welcome to the vibrant city of **Brisbane**, nestled on the eastern coast of Australia. This travel guide book is your key to unlocking the wonders and adventures that await you in this remarkable city. Whether you're a first-time visitor or a seasoned traveler, this comprehensive guide will provide you with all the information you need to make the most of your time in Brisbane.

Brisbane is a cosmopolitan metropolis that combines a modern urban landscape with stunning natural beauty. From its iconic landmarks to its lively cultural scene, there is something for everyone in this city. Explore the South Bank Parklands, a vibrant hub of entertainment, dining, and outdoor activities. Take a leisurely stroll along the scenic Brisbane River and discover the city's rich history and architecture. Immerse yourself in the local arts and culture at the Queensland Cultural Centre, home to world-class museums, galleries, and theaters.

But don't just take our word for it. Let us introduce you to Sarah, an avid traveler who recently used this guide to explore Brisbane. Sarah arrived in Brisbane armed with the knowledge and recommendations provided in this travel guide book. She followed the suggested itineraries, visiting the city's must-see attractions and hidden gems.

From the panoramic views atop the Story Bridge to the vibrant energy of the West End neighborhood, Sarah experienced the city like a true local.

With the guide's practical tips and insider knowledge, Sarah effortlessly navigated Brisbane's public transportation system, savored the local cuisine at recommended restaurants, and connected with the friendly locals. She felt confident and well-prepared, making the most of her time in the city and creating memories that would last a lifetime.

Now, it's your turn to embark on your own Brisbane adventure. Let this guide be your trusty companion, guiding you through the city's diverse neighborhoods, revealing its cultural treasures, and providing you with invaluable insights to ensure a remarkable and unforgettable journey. So, pack your bags, open this guide, and get ready to explore the wonders of Brisbane, Australia's hidden gem on the eastern coast.

Chapter One

Getting to Know Brisbane

Overview of Brisbane

Brisbane, the capital of Queensland, is a vibrant city nestled on the eastern coast of Australia. Brisbane is said to be the third largest city in Australia with over 2,500,000 people. Brisbane offers a unique blend of modern urban landscapes, natural beauty, and a laid-back lifestyle. The city is divided by the meandering Brisbane River, with a thriving central business district on one side and a plethora of cultural and recreational attractions on the other.

History and Culture

Brisbane has a rich history that dates back thousands of years, with the area originally inhabited by Indigenous Australians. European settlement began in the early 19th century, and Brisbane quickly developed into a bustling river port. Today, the city celebrates its cultural heritage through various museums, art galleries, and festivals. Visitors can explore the Queensland

Museum and Gallery of Modern Art to delve into the region's history and contemporary arts scene.

Climate and Best Time to Visit

Brisbane enjoys a subtropical climate with warm summers and mild winters. The city experiences a high level of sunshine throughout the year, making it an ideal destination for outdoor activities. The best time to visit Brisbane is during the spring (September to November) and autumn (March to May) seasons when temperatures are pleasant, and the city hosts a range of events and festivals. However, it's worth noting that Brisbane can be prone to heavy rainfall during the summer months (December to February).

Getting Around Brisbane

Brisbane offers a well-connected public transportation system, making it easy for visitors to navigate the city. The TransLink network includes buses, trains, and ferries, providing convenient access to various neighborhoods and attractions. The CityCat and CityFerry services offer a scenic way to explore the city along the Brisbane River. For those who prefer to drive, Brisbane has an extensive road network, and car rentals are readily available. Cycling is also a popular option, with numerous bike paths and rental services throughout the city.

Safety and Emergency Information

Brisbane is generally a safe city for travelers, but it's always important to take necessary precautions. The emergency number in Australia is **000** for immediate assistance in case of emergencies. It is advisable to stay aware of your surroundings, especially in busy areas, and keep belongings secure. It's also essential to protect yourself from the sun's strong rays by wearing sunscreen, a hat, and staying hydrated.

In the event of any emergency, Brisbane has excellent healthcare facilities, including public and private hospitals. It is recommended that visitors have travel insurance to cover any medical expenses during their stay. It's also worth noting that Brisbane has a high-quality tap water supply, so there's no need to buy bottled water.

By familiarizing yourself with Brisbane's history, climate, transportation options, and safety measures, you can confidently explore the city and make the most of your time in this captivating destination. So, get ready to immerse yourself in the rich culture and inviting atmosphere of Brisbane, where memorable experiences await at every turn.

9

Chapter Two

Exploring Brisbane

Brisbane, the capital city of Queensland, Australia, is a vibrant and diverse destination offering a wide range of attractions and activities for visitors to explore. From its bustling city center to its cultural and historical sites, nature and outdoor activities, dining and nightlife, and shopping and markets, Brisbane has something to offer everyone. Let's delve into the various facets of this exciting city.

1. City Center and Central Business District (CBD)

The city center and Central Business District (CBD) of Brisbane are the beating heart of the city. Here, you'll find a mix of towering skyscrapers, historic buildings, shopping precincts, and lively entertainment areas. The CBD is easily accessible and serves as a convenient starting point for exploring the city.

2. Queen Street Mall

Queen Street Mall is Brisbane's premier shopping destination. This pedestrian mall spans several blocks and is lined with a plethora of shops, boutiques, department stores, and eateries. It's a bustling hub where locals and tourists alike gather to shop, dine, and enjoy street performances.

3. South Bank Parklands

Located on the southern bank of the Brisbane River, South Bank Parklands is a vibrant recreational area that offers a mix of lush gardens, promenades, restaurants, and cultural attractions. Visitors can relax by the man-made Streets Beach, explore the Queensland Cultural Centre, visit the Queensland Art Gallery and Gallery of Modern Art (QAGOMA), or enjoy a picnic in the beautiful parklands.

4. Kangaroo Point

Kangaroo Point, situated just across the river from the CBD, offers stunning views of the city skyline and is a popular spot for outdoor enthusiasts. The area features scenic cliffs, riverside parks, and walking and cycling paths. Adventure seekers can also try rock climbing or abseiling down the cliffs.

5. Cultural and Historical Sites

Brisbane is rich in cultural and historical sites that provide insight into the city's past and present.

6. Brisbane City Hall

Brisbane City Hall is an iconic landmark that dominates the city's skyline. This grand building, built in the 1920s, houses the Museum of Brisbane, which showcases the history and art of the city. Visitors can take guided tours to learn about the building's architecture and explore the museum's exhibitions.

7. Queensland Museum and Sciencentre

The Queensland Museum and Sciencentre is a must-visit for those interested in natural history, science, and interactive exhibits. The museum offers engaging displays on the region's natural environment, indigenous cultures, and prehistoric creatures. The Sciencentre is a hands-on discovery zone that encourages visitors to explore scientific concepts through interactive displays and experiments.

8. The Story Bridge

The Story Bridge is an iconic Brisbane landmark that spans the Brisbane River, connecting the CBD with Kangaroo Point. Visitors can take guided tours to learn about the bridge's construction and history or enjoy panoramic views of the city by climbing to the top of the bridge's steel structure on the Story Bridge Adventure Climb.

9. Nature and Outdoor Activities

Brisbane is known for its abundant natural beauty and outdoor recreational opportunities.

10. Lone Pine Koala Sanctuary

This is the largest and the first koala sanctuary in the world. Located on the banks of the Brisbane River, it is home to a wide variety of Australian wildlife, including koalas, kangaroos, wombats, and platypuses. Visitors can cuddle a koala, hand-feed kangaroos, and watch exciting wildlife shows.

11. Mount Coot-tha

For breathtaking views of Brisbane and its surrounding areas, head to Mount Coot-tha. This mountain is located west of the city and offers several walking trails, picnic areas, and the popular Mount Coot-tha Botanic Gardens. The summit also features the Sir Thomas Brisbane Planetarium, where visitors can explore the wonders of the universe through interactive displays and astronomical shows.

12. Moreton Island

Moreton Island, located just off the coast of Brisbane, is a paradise for nature lovers. The island is renowned for its crystal-clear waters, pristine beaches, and diverse marine life. Visitors can go snorkeling or scuba diving around the Tangalooma Wrecks, explore the island's sand dunes on a 4WD adventure, or relax and unwind in the natural beauty of the surroundings.

13. Dining and Nightlife

Brisbane offers a vibrant dining and nightlife scene with a wide range of options to suit every taste and preference.

14. Fortitude Valley

Fortitude Valley, often referred to as "The Valley," is a trendy inner-city suburb known for its eclectic mix of restaurants, bars, nightclubs, and live music venues. It's a popular destination for those seeking a lively and vibrant night out on the town.

15. Eagle Street Pier

Eagle Street Pier is a waterfront precinct located in the CBD, offering a selection of fine dining restaurants, cocktail bars, and riverfront views. It's a great place to enjoy a leisurely lunch, indulge in a romantic dinner, or simply relax with a drink while taking in the scenic beauty of the Brisbane River.

16. Eat Street Northshore

For a unique dining experience, head to Eat Street Northshore. This vibrant night market is housed in a converted shipping container terminal and features a vast array of international cuisine, dessert stalls, and bars. It's a food lover's paradise where you can savor flavors from around the world while enjoying live entertainment.

17. Shopping and Markets

Brisbane offers a diverse shopping experience, from modern malls to bustling markets.

18. Queen Street Mall

As mentioned earlier, Queen Street Mall is a prime shopping destination in Brisbane, offering a wide range of retail outlets, fashion boutiques, department stores, and specialty shops. It's the perfect place to indulge in some retail therapy and find the latest fashion trends.

19. James Street

James Street, located in the inner-city suburb of Fortitude Valley, is a trendy precinct known for its upscale fashion boutiques, designer homewares, and gourmet food stores. It's a haven for fashionistas and those seeking unique and high-quality products.

20. South Bank Lifestyle Markets

The South Bank Lifestyle Markets, held on the weekends, offer a vibrant atmosphere and a variety of stalls selling fashion, accessories, arts and crafts, and delicious street food. Located in the heart of South Bank, these markets are a great place to browse for unique souvenirs or sample local cuisine.

In conclusion, Brisbane is a dynamic and exciting city that offers a wide range of attractions and activities. From its bustling city center and cultural landmarks to its natural beauty and vibrant dining scene, there is something for everyone to enjoy in this cosmopolitan Australian destination.

Chapter Three

Day Trips from Brisbane

Brisbane, with its central location in Queensland, Australia, serves as an excellent base for exploring the surrounding regions. From stunning beaches to lush rainforests, there are several exciting day trip destinations near Brisbane that offer diverse experiences. Let's dive into some of the most popular day trip options to try:

1. Gold Coast

The Gold Coast, located just south of Brisbane, is renowned for its beautiful beaches, vibrant nightlife, and world-class theme parks. Surfers Paradise is the heart of the Gold Coast, where visitors can soak up the sun, catch a wave, or stroll along the bustling esplanade. Theme park enthusiasts can spend a day at Movie World, Sea World, or Wet'n'Wild. Additionally, the Gold Coast hinterland offers breathtaking scenery, with national parks like Lamington and Springbrook showcasing lush rainforests, waterfalls, and walking trails.

2. Sunshine Coast

To the north of Brisbane lies the Sunshine Coast, a picturesque region known for its stunning beaches, charming coastal towns, and natural beauty. Noosa Heads is a popular destination within the Sunshine Coast, offering pristine beaches, a vibrant dining scene, and the iconic Noosa National Park. Visitors can enjoy coastal walks, spot wildlife, or relax on the golden sands. The Sunshine Coast is also home to the Australia Zoo, made famous by the late Steve Irwin, where visitors can get up close with native wildlife and learn about conservation efforts.

3. Byron Bay

For a laid-back and bohemian atmosphere, head south to Byron Bay in New South Wales. This coastal town is renowned for its alternative lifestyle, beautiful beaches, and surf culture. Byron Bay's Cape Byron Lighthouse, situated on the easternmost point of Australia, offers panoramic views of the Pacific Ocean and is a popular spot for whale watching during migration seasons.

The town itself is a hub of unique shops, cafes, and wellness retreats, making it a favorite among artists, surfers, and those seeking a relaxed coastal getaway.

4. Lamington National Park

Lamington National Park, located in the hinterland between Brisbane and the Gold Coast, is a paradise for nature lovers and outdoor enthusiasts. The park is part of the Gondwana Rainforests of Australia World Heritage Area, boasting ancient rainforests, cascading waterfalls, and diverse wildlife. Visitors can embark on scenic hikes, explore the treetop canopy walkways at O'Reilly's Rainforest Retreat, or spot rare bird species, including the vibrant and elusive Albert's lyrebird.

5. Noosa Heads

Noosa Heads, situated within the Sunshine Coast region, deserves special mention as a popular day trip destination from Brisbane. This coastal town is famous for its pristine beaches, national parks, and sophisticated dining scene. Noosa Main Beach is a favorite among surfers and sunbathers, while Noosa National Park offers picturesque coastal walks with the chance to spot koalas and dolphins. The Noosa River is perfect for water activities such as kayaking, stand-up paddleboarding, and boat tours. Noosa Heads also boasts an array of high-end restaurants and trendy boutiques along Hastings Street, catering to discerning visitors.

To sum it all, Brisbane serves as an excellent base for exploring the surrounding regions, with a variety of enticing day trip options. Whether you choose to venture to the vibrant Gold Coast, serene Sunshine Coast, bohemian Byron Bay, nature-rich Lamington National Park, or sophisticated Noosa Heads, each destination offers its own unique charm and experiences, ensuring an unforgettable day trip from Brisbane.

Chapter Four

Accommodation Options

When visiting Brisbane, there are various accommodation options to suit every traveler's preferences and budget. From luxurious hotels and resorts to budget-friendly hostels and the convenience of apartment rentals, Brisbane offers a diverse range of choices for a comfortable and enjoyable stay.

Hotels and Resorts

Brisbane boasts a wide selection of hotels and resorts, catering to different tastes and providing a range of amenities and services. From luxurious five-star establishments to boutique hotels and well-known international chains, there is no shortage of options for those seeking a refined and pampering experience. Many hotels in Brisbane are located in the CBD or near popular attractions, providing convenient access to the city's highlights. Guests can expect well-appointed rooms, on-site dining options, fitness centers, swimming pools, spas, and attentive service. Whether it's a business trip, a romantic getaway, or a family vacation,

Brisbane's hotels and resorts offer a comfortable and indulgent stay.

Hostels and Budget Accommodation

For budget-conscious travelers, hostels and budget accommodation provide affordable and sociable options. Brisbane has a range of hostels scattered throughout the city, particularly in areas popular with backpackers and young travelers. These accommodations often offer shared dormitory-style rooms with shared facilities such as kitchens and common areas. Hostels provide an opportunity to meet fellow travelers, share experiences, and make new friends. While the emphasis is on affordability, many hostels also prioritize cleanliness, security, and a lively atmosphere. Some hostels even offer private rooms for those seeking more privacy while still enjoying the social aspect of hostel living.

Apartment Rentals

Apartment rentals provide a flexible and home-like accommodation option for visitors to Brisbane. Renting an apartment is an excellent choice for families, larger groups, or those looking for a longer-term stay.

Brisbane offers a variety of serviced apartments and vacation rentals in different neighborhoods, allowing guests to experience the city like a local. Apartments are fully furnished, providing separate bedrooms, living areas, and kitchen facilities, offering the comforts and convenience of a home away from home. This option gives travelers the flexibility to cook their meals, enjoy additional living space, and have a more immersive experience in the city. Apartment rentals are particularly advantageous for those who value independence, privacy, and the ability to live like a local.

Brisbane provides a diverse range of accommodation options to suit different needs and preferences. Whether you're looking for luxury and indulgence in hotels and resorts, a budget-friendly and social experience in hostels, or the flexibility and comfort of apartment rentals, Brisbane has something for everyone. With its array of accommodation choices, visitors to Brisbane can find the perfect place to relax and recharge, ensuring a memorable and enjoyable stay in the city.

Chapter Five

Practical Information

When planning a trip to Brisbane, it's essential to have some practical information to make your visit smooth and enjoyable. From transportation options and local cuisine to shopping tips, language and communication, and health and safety considerations, here is a comprehensive guide to help you navigate your way through the city.

Transportation

Brisbane offers a range of transportation options to help you get around the city:

- **Public Transportation:** Brisbane has an extensive public transportation network consisting of buses, trains, and ferries operated by TransLink. The go card is a reusable smart card that allows for easy payment and discounted fares across all modes of public transport.

- **CityCat Ferries:** The CityCat is a popular mode of transportation that operates along the Brisbane River, offering scenic views of the city. It's a convenient way to explore different parts of Brisbane, including South Bank and New Farm.

- **Taxis and Ride-Sharing Services:** Taxis are readily available in the city, and ride-sharing services like Uber are also widely used. Just be aware that fares may vary depending on demand and traffic conditions.

- **Cycling:** Brisbane has an extensive network of cycling paths, making it a bike-friendly city. You can rent bicycles from various locations or make use of the city's bike-sharing program, CityCycle.

Local Cuisine and Restaurants

Brisbane is known for its diverse culinary scene, offering a wide range of local and international cuisines. Some popular local dishes and specialties to try include:

- **Moreton Bay Bugs:** These are a type of seafood native to the waters around Brisbane, similar to lobster or crayfish. They are often grilled or served in seafood platters.

- **Australian Beef:** Australia is renowned for its high-quality beef, so be sure to try a juicy steak or a classic Aussie beef pie.

- **Pavlova:** A popular dessert in Australia, Pavlova is a meringue-based cake topped with fresh fruits and whipped cream.

Brisbane has a multitude of restaurants, cafes, and street food stalls catering to various tastes and budgets. You can find everything from fine dining establishments to casual eateries offering international cuisines. Popular dining precincts include South Bank, Fortitude Valley, and Eagle Street Pier.

Shopping Tips

If you enjoy shopping, Brisbane offers a variety of options:
- **Queen Street Mall:** This pedestrian mall in the CBD is a shopper's paradise, featuring numerous retail stores, department stores, and boutiques.
- **Fortitude Valley:** Known for its eclectic mix of fashion boutiques, vintage stores, and unique shops, Fortitude Valley is a trendy shopping destination.
- **Markets:** Brisbane is home to various markets where you can find local produce, arts and crafts, fashion, and more. Some popular markets include the South Bank Lifestyle Markets, Eagle Farm Markets, and Davies Park Market.

Language and Communication

English is the official language spoken in Brisbane and throughout Australia. Communication should not be a barrier for English-speaking visitors. However, if English is not your first language, you may still find people who speak different languages in the city due to its multicultural nature.

Health and Safety

Brisbane is generally a safe city to visit, but it's always important to take standard precautions:

- **Health:** Ensure you have travel insurance that covers any medical expenses. Brisbane has excellent medical facilities and pharmacies if needed.

- **Safety:** While Brisbane is relatively safe, it's advisable to take precautions against theft and pickpocketing. Be cautious of your belongings, particularly in crowded areas or public transport. It's also recommended to stay aware of your surroundings, especially at night, and use well-lit and busy areas.

- **Emergency Services:** Incase of emergencies, dial 000 for immediate assistance from the police, fire department, or ambulance service.

In addition, being aware of practical information when visiting Brisbane can enhance your experience and ensure a smooth and enjoyable trip. Understanding transportation options, exploring the local cuisine, knowing where to shop, being familiar with the language and communication, and prioritizing health and safety considerations will help you make the best of your time in this beautiful city.

Conclusion

Brisbane, with its captivating blend of urban sophistication and natural beauty, offers a truly unforgettable experience for visitors. From its vibrant city center and bustling Central Business District to its cultural and historical landmarks, stunning nature and outdoor activities, diverse dining and nightlife scene, and fantastic shopping options, Brisbane has something to captivate every traveler.

Final Thoughts

As you explore the city, you'll be enthralled by the iconic Queen Street Mall, the tranquil South Bank Parklands, and the breathtaking views from Kangaroo Point. Immerse yourself in the rich cultural heritage of Brisbane City Hall, delve into the wonders of science at the Queensland Museum and Sciencentre, and admire the majestic Story Bridge. Indulge in encounters with adorable koalas at the Lone Pine Koala Sanctuary, soak in the panoramic vistas from Mount Coot-tha, and discover the paradise of Moreton Island.

When it comes to dining and nightlife, Fortitude Valley will entice you with its trendy vibe, Eagle Street Pier will enchant you with its waterfront charm, and Eat Street Northshore will tantalize your taste buds with its diverse culinary delights. And for those seeking retail therapy, the Queen Street Mall, James Street, and the South Bank Lifestyle Markets offer an array of shopping experiences.

Safe Trip !!!

Use the note journal provided at the end of this book to write down your travel experience.

Travel Tracker Notebook
Journal

_____

_____

_____

_____

_____

_____

_____

_____

_____

_____

_____

_____